The Caregiver's Book
Caring for Another, Caring for Yourself

Text and Photography by
James E. Miller

WILL☘WGREEN®
PUBLISHING

To my sister, Patty Lee, with love.

ACKNOWLEDGMENTS

Several friends and colleagues have helped in the development of ideas for this book. Connie Croyle, Kay Roberts, Roxandra Clemmons-McFarthing, Clare Barton, Jennifer Levine, John Peterson, Bernie Miller, and Ron Williams each added thoughts and insights. Jennifer Levine and Patty Lee generously shared their ideas for the Suggestions pages. Katherine Misegades provided the graphic design. This book is, in every way, a collaboration.

Library of Congress Control Number 2008933767

ISBN 978-1885933-41-6

10351 Dawson's Creek Boulevard, Suite B
Fort Wayne, Indiana 46825
260.490.2222
www.willowgreen.com

Foreword

Caregiving. The word brings to mind beautiful images of compassion and self-sacrifice: cradling a newborn, comforting someone who is ill or dying, supporting the bereaved. Healthy caregiving can bring out all that is best in us. And that is beautiful.

But there is another side to caregiving. Done without rest or relief, caregiving becomes a chore and a drain. Done without adequate knowledge and support, it can become confusing and harrowing. Done without appreciation and understanding, it can turn disappointing and disheartening.

Most people are not prepared for all that the caregiving role demands. When my wife developed cancer and I became her caregiver, I went into the experience with high hopes and good intentions and then discovered that I lacked something—something critical. Perhaps that's your experience too.

I hope you'll take your time as you read these pages. Reflect upon the quotations. Absorb the photographs. Try out the suggestions. Mostly, let this book help you step back to get a clearer, more accurate picture of your caregiving, to see in it an adventure you'll not forget and a privilege you'll come to cherish.

Jim Miller

Since you have chosen this book,

    or someone has chosen it for you,

        chances are you're a caregiver or about to become one.

Either way, you're aware that caregiving is a weighty matter.

Becoming responsible for another's care takes energy,

    and a lot of it.

It requires a combination of tenderness and firmness.

It's built upon self-discipline, self-confidence,

    and sometimes self-sacrifice.

Caregiving can ask of you courage and insight and perseverance.

As often as not, it's an extremely demanding role.

It's equally a terribly important role.

The one in your care may rely upon you for daily sustenance,

    physical comfort, a dose of encouragement.

You may be called upon to perform specialized procedures

    and to execute a host of other duties.

Caregiving never happens in a vacuum.

If you're caring for a family member or friend,

　　you have other responsibilities in your life as well,

　　　　and probably many other concerns.

If you're a professional caregiver,

　　you have the pressures of patient loads, paperwork, and protocols,

　　　　not to mention all the relationships involved,

　　　　　　quite apart from your own challenges in life.

To compound the situation, you may have little or no training

　　in providing such personal attention to another human being.

Where is empathy taught?

Who is the instructor for setting boundaries?

How do you get a diploma in listening well?

Questions like these point eventually to another question:

How do you provide care that is healthy—

　　healthy for the other and for yourself at the same time?

This book provides a few ideas about wise caregiving.

It's designed to meet the needs of those who are busy with chores,

those who feel the weight of these responsibilities.

Eight general ideas will be presented

with specific suggestions growing out of each.

There will also be photographs for you to ponder,

and wisdom from the ages for you to fathom.

Words will be kept to a minimum,

so your thoughts and feelings will have room to roam.

As you'll see by making your way through these pages,

caregiving is not all duty and demands.

Caregiving can also be a fulfilling opportunity,

a wonderful adventure, a marvelous privilege.

It can become an unspeakable grace.

If you have not discovered that already, you will.

THE HEALTHIEST WAY TO CARE FOR ANOTHER
IS TO CARE FOR YOURSELF.

The needs of the person entrusted to your care

    are very important to you.

If they're ill or in pain, if they're frightened or upset,

    you want to ease their discomfort, to soothe their feelings.

If they're facing long-term limitations or long-suffering decline,

    you want to provide supportive assistance,

        and in the manner they desire.

You are in a position to make a real difference in their life.

You can be mature enough and unselfish enough

    to put their interests ahead of your own.

You can be gracious enough to help them even when you're tired,

    to encourage them even when you feel low,

        to pamper them even when you'd like to be pampered yourself.

But, without being fully aware of what you're doing,

    and still for the best of reasons,

        you can at the same time endanger your caregiving.

Help thyself, and God will help thee.

George Herbert

Love is not a possession but a growth.
The heart is a lamp with just enough oil to burn for an hour,
and if there be no oil to put in again, its light will go out.

Henry Ward Beecher

I am only one,
but I am still one.
I cannot do everything,
but I can do something;
and because I cannot do everything
I will not refuse to do the something that I can do.

Edward Everett Hale

When caring for another becomes a significant part

of how you spend your days,

then caring for yourself becomes equally important.

In order to give, you must have something within you to give.

In order to share your strength,

you must have ways to marshal that strength.

In order to offer something fresh to the one who so needs it,

you must make sure you have ways to be refreshed yourself.

Self-care is not a matter of selfishness or unselfishness.

It's a matter of encouraging your own vitality

and replenishing your own resources,

so you can give your most beneficial and wholesome care

to someone who needs it.

No matter how encompassing the other person's needs,

you have needs that are no less important.

For your sake, and for the other's sake,

your needs as a human being deserve attention too.

Begin by becoming aware of your personal needs,

    just as you're aware of the needs of the one you're caring for.

Then work to satisfy those.

Find ways to get the rest you cannot do without,

    however strong you are,

        however loving you feel.

Maintain your energy by eating and drinking healthfully.

Build your stamina with regular exercise.

Set aside time each day just for yourself.

Open yourself to healing influences all around you—

    in nature and in other people,

        through art and music and literature,

            with practices that quiet you and center you.

Give yourself opportunities for fun.

Indulge yourself now and again, remembering you're worth it.

Always remember: only by caring for yourself

    can you adequately, consistently provide healthy care for another.

Heal yourself first before you heal others.

African proverb

*Renew yourself completely each day;
do it again, and again, and forever again.*

Chinese inscription cited by
Henry David Thoreau

*Take care of your body with steadfast fidelity.
The soul must see through these eyes alone,
and if they are dim, the whole world is clouded.*

Johann Wolfgang von Goethe

List things you can do for yourself.

What are those things? Take a long hot bath? Order out Chinese food? Read that mystery novel? Make a long list of favorite activities that restore you. Put the list where you'll see it often. If you're not doing some of those activities daily, remind yourself how important your self-care is. Then be kind and do something wonderful for yourself that very day. And every day after.

Develop a plan for respite care.

Make sure you get away for short breaks. If you're a family caregiver, be proactive about creating such times. When someone says, "Let me know if I can do anything to help," take them up on their offer. See if there is an adult day-care center in your community or perhaps part-time home-care services. From time to time plan a longer period away.

Celebrate "unbirthdays."

For no reason at all, and for the best of reasons, throw an all-day "unbirthday" party occasionally. Do it for yourself as much as for the one in your care. Put up decorations. Wrap little gifts. Arrange a bouquet of flowers. Dress up. Eat a special meal. Play celebrative music. Have an "unbirthday" cake, of course. Whoop it up. Go to bed that night with a smile on your face.

BY FOCUSING ON YOUR FEELINGS,
YOU CAN FOCUS BEYOND YOUR FEELINGS.

You may have thought that, as a caregiver,

you're supposed to do whatever is required of you

without letting your emotions get involved.

That expectation is unfair and unhealthy,

for genuine caregiving involves your whole self—

including your emotions.

Caregiving naturally activates so much inside you:

concern for what's happening to the person you care for;

feelings about that person as a human being;

responses to others with whom you interact;

anticipation about what lies ahead.

Your feelings can help you get a clearer sense

of what's going on all around you.

So don't hide your feelings or ignore them.

Explore them.

Value them.

Better to be without logic than without feeling.

Charlotte Brontë

Seeing is believing,
but feeling is God's own truth.

Irish proverb

Never apologize for showing feeling.
When you do so, you apologize for truth.

Benjamin Disraeli

Respect in yourself the oscillation of feelings;
they are your life and your nature;
a wiser than you made them.

Henri Amiel

A cardinal rule for caregivers is this:

    feel whatever it is you feel,

        and feel it as fully as you can.

The range of feelings you may experience is vast.

You may fear you cannot do all it appears you must do.

At times you may feel more weary than you wish,

    more anxious than you'd like to admit,

        more saddened than you'd want to express.

You may feel frustrated for any number of reasons—

    or resentful, or bitter, or even furious.

You may feel sorry for yourself, or for the one in your care,

    or for both of you together.

Then again, you may feel pleased you're able to do what you can.

You may be proud of what you're accomplishing together.

You may be grateful for blessings both large and small.

You may feel great love.

At times you may experienced unqualified joy.

Remember that all your feelings are valid,

all are worth your attention and your expression.

For in the act of drawing out what is inside yourself,

wonderful things can happen.

You can learn and grow.

You can become more free, more sure, more whole.

So find someone you can talk to and give your feelings a voice.

Be open to releasing your feelings in other ways, too.

You may cry them, or laugh them, or pray them.

You may write them, or sing them, or paint them.

You may intentionally mull your feelings, silently yet surely.

Don't be surprised if your feelings conflict with one another.

That's not unusual when so much is going on

inside and outside of you.

By focusing on your emotions,

and by freeing them in ways best suited to you,

you can help ensure that your feelings do not get in the way

of your caregiving.

*It is not a matter of thinking a great deal
but of loving a great deal,
so do whatever arouses you most to love.*

Teresa of Avila

*We know the truth, not only by reason,
but also by the heart.*

Blaise Pascal

*For the human soul is hospitable, and will entertain
conflicting sentiments and contradictory opinions
with much impartiality.*

Mary Ann Evans

Suggestions

Find someone with whom you can honestly share your feelings.

Every caregiver deserves the opportunity to open up to another human being. Speaking your feelings to another is a way of unbottling them. It helps you get a better perspective about your role. You can learn certain things about your emotions, too—how they change, how they can be both predictable and surprising. Just make sure the listener is not the one you're caring for; you need someone more objective.

Journal.

Write about what's going on in your life, including what's happening inside—your feelings, insights, and reflections. Try doing this daily, or at least several times a week. Find a comfortable place that's both quiet and private. Write in a notebook if you prefer, or tap away on a keyboard. Every so often, read back through your entries. Ask yourself, "What am I learning? How am I growing?"

Let off steam physically.

Even if your caregiving involves plenty of physical exercise, it helps to set aside time for those activities that honor your body and help clear your mind. What works for you? Aerobics? Swimming? Yoga? Tai chi? Jogging? Brisk walks? Some people like to vacuum with a vengeance. Others enjoy group sports. Keeping your body in shape is a good way to help keep your mind in shape. You'll be a better person and a better caregiver for it.

To be close, you must establish boundaries.

When the needs of someone you care for are great,

    or when you've become part of the other's life in so many ways,

        you may desire to draw as close as possible.

You may be inclined to keep that person

    always at the forefront of your thoughts,

        always within easy reach of their grasp.

Intentionally or unintentionally, you may act as if

    you're the only person who can be of help,

        or should be of help.

You may find yourself almost merging with that other person,

    so whatever happens to them happens to you.

Whatever they feel, you feel.

Whatever their pain, you take it on as your own.

Identifying so completely with another

    is an ideal some caregivers have sought.

But it is less than ideal.

*The sense of dignity grows
with the ability to say no.*

Abraham Joshua Heschel

*Love consists in this:
that two solitudes protect and border and salute each other.*

Rainer Maria Rilke

*There are three things that if people do not know,
they cannot live long in this world:
what is too much for them,
what is too little for them,
and what is just right for them.*

Swahili proverb

To be a good caregiver, you must maintain your separateness.

While you may care deeply for that other person,

    you are still your own unique self.

You have your own life to claim.

And that includes having your own limits to set.

There are times when it's appropriate to say "no,"

    however much you care,

        and even because you care.

There are times when it makes good sense to guard your privacy,

    to protect your energy,

        to preserve your other relationships.

There are times when it's natural to give yourself a reprieve

    by asking another to help you,

        or to be there in your place.

In recognizing that at times you feel overloaded or overwhelmed,

    and in being responsible to act to correct that,

        you will be doing the most caring thing possible.

By establishing boundaries about what you're prepared and able to do,

and when, and where, and how, and why,

you can help the one you're caring for,

while taking care of yourself.

You'll be able to see more clearly

what's happening in this relationship and what isn't,

what's needed and what's possible.

And by creating a separate space for yourself,

you'll help ensure that the one you care for

will have *their* own separate space.

They need it as much as you—perhaps even more.

For they may not have the strength or clarity

to create that space on their own.

Once you have established clear boundaries,

you can approach one another with a freedom and an honesty,

with an objectivity and a directness,

that would not otherwise happen.

And you can be the closer for having stayed apart.

Good fences make good neighbors.

Robert Frost

*The excessively kind-hearted person
becomes a slave.*

Burmese proverb

The one who helps everybody, helps nobody.

Spanish proverb

*It is love that asks, that seeks,
that knocks, that finds,
and that is faithful in what it finds.*

Augustine of Hippo

SUGGESTIONS

Create a "time out" sign and use it.

Sometimes you don't feel like talking or being bothered. Everyone has those times. Communicate your legitimate desire in a friendly, visible manner. Wear a particular hat or tuck something in your shirt pocket that serves as a signal. Encourage the one in your care to have their own "time out" sign. Being able to create these islands of solitude without offending the other person can be a lifesaver.

Define your limits.

Everyone has things they cannot or should not do in their caregiving. How much should you lift? How long can you stay awake? How cheerful can you be before your morning coffee? Be clear about what you're able and willing to do. Be just as clear about what you will not do. If it's appropriate, let the one in your care know your limits. Give thought to how you can honor your limits while seeing that the other person is adequately cared for. Trust others to assist you.

Carve out your own space.

If you're a family caregiver, carve out an area that is yours, either in the same room where you do your caregiving or another room. Design it to suit your tastes. Include whatever feels comfortable and homey—pictures, books and magazines, family mementos, writing supplies, something from nature. What about treating yourself to something special—a piece of artwork or a music system? Caring for your surroundings can be an important way of caring for yourself.

IN ACCEPTING YOUR HELPLESSNESS, YOU BECOME A BETTER HELPER.

One reason you're a caregiver is you believe you can make a difference.

You want to play a role in correcting what may have gone awry.

You want to assure and comfort, protect and provide.

In a word, you want to help.

There is a difficult double lesson any caregiver will do well to learn.

One lesson is, no matter how much you do to help,

 there is still much you cannot do.

The other's pain cannot be absorbed or taken away.

The other's mending can be neither hurried nor circumvented.

And if they must accept these things, so must you.

Sometimes the other's condition will not improve,

 no matter what you do.

Sometimes what you have to offer is not accepted,

 and you are powerless to give what you have to give.

The more you come to know what your caregiving can accomplish,

 the more you also come to know what it cannot accomplish.

The sun will set without your assistance.

Hebrew proverb

Life is a teacher in the art of relinquishing.

Socrates

*Our letting go is in order
that God might be God in us.*

Meister Eckhart

*Sometimes it is more important
to discover what we cannot do,
than what we can do.*

Lin Yutang

Another difficult lesson to learn is this:

 however much care you can provide,

  it may not be the amount of care, or the kind of care,

   you *should* provide.

Caregivers sometimes try to do too much.

Out of your own needs,

 or out of your own unknowing,

  you may move to do what someone else is better suited to do.

Perhaps there is another who needs or deserves

 to be by that person's side,

  in addition to you, or instead of you.

Just as important, perhaps the "someone" who needs to do more

 is the one you are caring for.

It may be that she or he will benefit

 from having less done rather than more,

  for their own strength or self-esteem or integrity.

There is a price that goes with being too dependent.

Sometimes caregivers, in their desire to help, can forget that.

As you come to accept the ways you cannot and should not help,

　you open opportunities for genuine caregiving to happen.

You permit yourself to do what is uniquely yours to do:

　to be really with the person you're caring for,

　　side by side, heart to heart.

You free yourself to help create an environment

　in which healing can begin to take place on its own,

　　whether that healing is physical, emotional, or spiritual—

　　　or all of these.

By acknowledging there is much beyond your ability and control,

　you make room for the unfolding of that healing potential

　　which is miraculously built into every human being.

You help shape that sacred space

　in which people can meet at a deeper level,

　　where relationships can be redeemed, and love can be rekindled.

In other words, you can move out of the way

　and allow the Source of All Life to be the source of all life.

In doing so, you fulfill your caregiver calling in yet another way.

We can do noble acts
without ruling earth and sea.

Aristotle

Learn to live in the passive voice
and let life be willed through you.

Thomas Kelly

Not being able to govern events,
I govern myself.

Michel de Montaigne

God is our refuge and strength, a very present help in trouble.
Therefore we will not fear, though the earth should change,
though the mountains shake in the heart of the sea.

Psalm 46:1-2

Inspect your feelings of helplessness.

Valuable information is here. What are these times like for you? What brings on these times? Do other feelings emerge too? Which ones? Can you recall any times early in your life when you felt powerless? How did you respond? What has helped you get through such times in the past? Don't stop your delving without asking, "What is the grace that has accompanied my helplessness?"

Learn how others have coped with powerlessness.

You may benefit from reading about others' experiences. Wendy Lustbader's *Counting on Kindness* helps explain what it's like for various caregivers. Maggie Strong's *Mainstay* describes what it was like for her as a spouse. *The Helper's Journey* by Dale Larson and *Witness to Illness* by Karen Horowitz and Douglas Lanes contain specific advice. Christopher Reeve's *Still Me* looks at helplessness from another perspective.

Communicate with the one in your care.

If your situation calls for it and your partner in care is open to it, talk about the idea that caregivers sometimes try to do too much. Ask them if this applies to you. Listen carefully and non-defensively if they answer affirmatively. Learn about specific incidents that serve as examples. Ask if they would benefit from doing more on their own. Discuss adjustments you each can make.

CAREGIVING IS MORE THAN GIVING CARE.
IT'S ALSO RECEIVING CARE.

Whether your caring is for someone who's long been a part of your life,

or for someone who is the recipient of the work you've chosen,

chances are you assumed your role with a particular idea in mind.

Someone needed care, you thought,

and you had care to give.

They should not have to go through this alone, you reasoned,

and you had companionship to offer,

which would surely help.

So you prepared to provide

and the other made ready to receive.

While a warm, caregiving relationship may begin this way,

it seldom ends this way.

True caregiving seldom goes in only one direction.

The hand that gives, gathers.

John Ray

Help thy brother's boat across, and lo!
thine own has reached the shore.

Indian proverb

There never was a person who did anything worth doing
that did not receive more than he gave.

Henry Ward Beecher

Blessed are those who give without remembering,
and take without forgetting.

Elizabeth Bibescoe

When you give from the depths of who you are,

    you do more than just give—you also gain.

When you reach out to another in this way,

    something comes back to you.

As for that person who receives your care—

    when they sense they're treated with respect and compassion,

        when they're valued for what *they* have to offer,

            they do much more than just receive.

They give as well.

They may give you their moral support,

    or gentle guidance,

        or quiet understanding.

They may offer you their wisdom, or cheer, or gratitude, or honesty.

They may bestow their insight or courage,

    their hope or their faith.

In short, they may, in their own way and in their own time,

    be a caregiver no less than you.

At its best, caregiving is more like *care sharing*.

It is a partnering that develops.

The two of you give, and find yourselves given to.

The two of you receive, and what you each receive is different,

    and it's what you each need.

Both of you are linked together,

    and an energy flows back and forth and back again.

There are times in that process

    when caregiving and care receiving fall away altogether.

When that happens, what remains is only you as people:

    two human beings who care for one another,

        who hope for one another,

            and who give thanks for one another.

And then caregiving becomes not a duty you do,

    but a grace you receive.

And care receiving becomes not a gift you passively accept,

    but a contribution you actively make.

Those whom we support hold us up in life.

Anne Sophie Swetchine

There are two ways of spreading light:
to be the candle, or the mirror that reflects it.

Edith Wharton

Some are reputed sick and some art not.
It often happens that the sicker man
is the nurse to the sounder.

Henry David Thoreau

We begin by imagining that we are giving to them;
we end by realizing that they have enriched us.

John Paul II

Record the gifts you receive from caregiving.

Keep a small notebook handy for jotting down your reflections. Write about those caregiving experiences that have brought you fulfillment or joy. Write also about those times when the one in your care has taught you or inspired you. When you discover something about yourself through this work of yours, include that. Note each gift caregiving brings, no matter how small. If it seems appropriate, talk about the gifts you've received with the one in your care.

Give your partner in care a thank-you gift.

Wrap up something meaningful for him or her. It needn't be a big gift—in fact, it shouldn't be. It might be something you make, or a treat you know they like, or something of your own you wish to share. Just make sure it's something you feel the other would appreciate. Be clear why you're offering this present—it's a token of your gratitude for what this person has added to your life.

Allow others to care for you.

Sometimes care is available from those around you: family members, friends, neighbors, colleagues, healthcare workers. An important thing you can do for these people, and for yourself, is to accept their care willingly and gratefully. Utilize their support. Bask in their affection. Enjoy their tribute. As you know, they can benefit from doing this, too.

As a caregiver, your strength is in your flexibility.

To be strong, it is often thought, is to remain firm.

To lead, it is often thought, means to have all the answers.

But genuine caregiving follows another set of rules.

Sometimes one must unlearn what seems right

    so one can relearn what works best.

And often what works best in caregiving

    has little to do with being strong in the traditional sense.

Often it's the opposite that works well—

    a readiness to bend and adapt,

        a willingness to be unsure at times.

There is wisdom in approaching your role with a beginner's mind,

    so you're always exploring, always learning.

Beginners are more likely to open to the possibilities

    than to cling to unchanging certainties.

If you stop to be kind,
you must swerve often from your path.

Mary Webb

You learn through mistakes—
no one was born a master.

Swiss proverb

Prepare yourself for the world
as the athletes used to do for their exercise;
oil your mind and your manners,
to give them the necessary suppleness and flexibility;
strength alone will not do.

Philip Stanhope

Everyone is unique.

You certainly are.

The person you care for undoubtedly is.

So is every family setting and every caregiving situation.

Therefore your task as an effective caregiver

    is to take all this uniqueness into account

        and respond sensitively, even creatively.

This will mean you'll probably do better as a caregiver

    with fewer rules rather than more.

You'll both profit from less emphasis on "right" ways and "wrong" ways,

    and more emphasis on understanding ways and loving ways.

Caregiving is not a time to try to be flawless.

It is a time to be flowing.

It is a time to express your strength through your gentleness,

    a time to be tender in your touch and in your talk,

        a time to be flexible in your interactions and expectations.

Almost a thousand years ago, a Tibetan named Milarepa

spoke words that every caregiver would do well to take to heart.

"Hasten slowly," he said, "that you may soon arrive."

Hasten slowly, as caregivers and care receivers,

that you may each reach the destination you seek,

and in the manner you each deserve.

Hasten slowly, and learn the practice of patience—

patience with the person you care for,

and patience with the one who's doing the caring.

Hasten slowly, and learn the art of forgiving,

as you look into one another's eyes,

and as you see your own image reflected there.

Hasten slowly, and learn the discipline of being sturdy enough to bend,

and firm enough to yield.

As you do so, your caregiving will assume a strength

it would not otherwise have.

*The wise adapt themselves to circumstances,
as water molds itself to the pitcher.*

Chinese proverb

*Be ever soft and pliable like a reed,
not hard and unbending like a cedar.*

The Talmud

*If you cannot go over,
you must go under.*

Yiddish proverb

*When I let go of what I am,
I become what I might be.*

Lao Tzu

SUGGESTIONS

Develop contingency plans.

Sometimes things will not go as you wish. Something unanticipated will happen to the one in your care or to your routines and plans. When that happens, you'll need new strategies. Make sure you've thought through options ahead of time. Know who the people are to whom you can turn. Create backup plans. Make sure someone else knows about these plans, too.

Learn how to brainstorm.

When you face a dilemma or difficulty, you'll probably have more ways of responding than you initially realize. Brainstorming can help. Start by listing options that easily come to mind. Write them down so you can see them. Add as many more as you can—funny and weird count, too. Ask others for their ideas. Build on one another's originality. Then go back through the list, eliminating what won't work, prioritizing what might work, and choosing what may work best.

Purposefully change your routine.

Shake things up by not doing your tasks at the same time in the same way. Reverse the order in which you do certain duties, if the order isn't important. Change the way you begin or end a task. Take a fresh-air break. Look for ways to add freshness and spontaneity to your role. That way you'll help minimize the effects of unplanned and necessary changes in the future. You'll be a veteran of flexibility long before you're called on to be.

THE ONLY WAY TO SUPPORT ANOTHER EFFECTIVELY IS TO BE EFFECTIVELY SUPPORTED.

However strong you are as a caregiver, your strength will run out.

You cannot perform continuously and indefinitely without support.

No one can.

However much patience and kindness you possess, you have limits.

Everyone does.

And even though you may know a great deal about

    caring for that other person,

        you don't know all there is to know about this care.

You *can't* know all there is to know.

This is not a matter of your intelligence or memory.

It has nothing to do with your motivation or devotion.

It has to do with your involvement and your perspective.

Some things are difficult to see when you're too close.

Some things are hard to sort out when there's so much to consider.

Some decisions are too far-reaching to make without outside input.

You need help.

You alone can do it, but you cannot do it alone.

O. Hobart Mowrer

Shared pain is half pain.

Dutch proverb

*What do we live for if not
to make life less difficult for each other?*

Mary Ann Evans

*No one is so rich that he does not need another's help;
no one so poor as not to be useful in some way
to his fellow man; and the disposition to ask assistance
from others with confidence, and to grant it with kindness,
is part of our very nature.*

Leo XIII

You would not want the one you're caring for to go without help.

Similarly, you dare not wish anything less for yourself.

You need your own opportunities to be nurtured and nourished.

You need your own freedom to express your feelings

without fear you'll offend the other.

You need the chance to learn how others have done

what is now yours to do.

You deserve to be around someone who will validate you,

someone who is interested, someone who will care.

If you're a part of a team of caregivers, so much the better.

You can open yourself to their viewpoints, insights, and favors.

If you're more alone in your role,

you might join a caregivers' support group in your community.

You might speak with a medical professional or mental health specialist,

a social worker or chaplain.

You might create your own caregiving team:

family and friends, neighbors and colleagues—anyone you trust.

Once your support system is in place, take advantage of it.

Accept graciously others' offers of assistance.

Learn to ask for what you need.

Make sure you have time off and time away,

and treat this time not as a luxury, but as what it is:

a human necessity.

Listen to those who are more experienced and borrow their ideas.

Find at least one person with whom you can really be yourself.

Figure out which people you can call upon at various times—

when you need to sound off, or when you need a good laugh;

when you need a steady shoulder,

or when you could use a pep talk.

Remember also that support is available on another plane.

At the very core of life itself,

you know the experience of being held invisibly,

making you aware that you are not alone.

You never have been.

Two-thirds of help is to give courage.

Irish proverb

*The hand of the stranger
is the hand of God.*

Gaelic proverb

*The delicate and infirm go for sympathy,
not to the well and buoyant,
but to those who have suffered like themselves.*

Catherine Esther Beecher

SUGGESTIONS

Join or start a caregiver support group.

If you're the primary caregiver for a family member or friend, you can benefit from talking honestly with people in similar situations. A support group can offer you encouragement and strength. Look for one through your local mental health center. Or call a hospital's social services department, a nearby hospice, or a 24-hour community help line. If you're a professional caregiver, meet with colleagues to talk about how you deal with your roles.

Join or start a caregiver co-op.

Sharing caregiving tasks with people in similar situations is a natural way to help and be helped. Share rides to doctor appointments or therapy sessions. Shop for one another or pick up prescriptions and medical supplies on a rotating basis. Stand in for one another so each caregiver can handle other responsibilities. Trade services. Cook for one another or eat together. Create your own community.

Locate support on the internet.

You can find support without leaving your chair. Communicate one-on-one or in small groups with fellow caregivers across town or around the world. Learn from professionals, reading what they've written; some will even respond to questions you pose. You can tap into vast amounts of information free of charge. You'll also find inspiration geared especially to caregivers—try *thoughtful-caregiver.com*.

**IN THE ORDINARINESS OF YOUR CAREGIVING
LIES SOMETHING MORE: SACREDNESS.**

Much about your caregiving revolves around the everyday.

It occurs in settings that are commonplace,

    among ordinary people who do ordinary things

        in very ordinary ways.

You have customary routines you follow,

    predictable tasks you perform,

        and, day in, day out, mundane details you attend to.

What could be more unremarkable?

Yet deep within all the ordinariness of your caregiving

    lies the real possibility of coming into contact

        with that which *is* remarkable:

            a sense of the sacred.

This can happen in various ways.

*Holy persons draw to themselves
all that is earthly.*

Hildegard of Bingen

*It is only by forgetting yourself
that you draw near to God.*

Henry David Thoreau

*To be really great in little things,
to be truly noble and heroic
in the insipid details of everyday life,
is a virtue so rare
as to be worthy of canonization.*

Harriet Beecher Stowe

As you engage in your very human acts of care,

   you may begin to witness signs of the Divine in your midst.

It can be seen in one another's face.

It can be felt in one another's touch.

It can be heard in one another's voice.

As you share the common stories of your lives,

   it's possible you can begin to see themes that are eternal

      and threads of the everlasting.

As you draw closer to one another in this partnership,

   you may find that you also draw closer to the One

      who is both far beyond and yet ever so near.

This caregiving ritual can take on a spiritual dimension in another way.

By being very present in each act of care,

   by being very conscious of the passing moments you share,

      you can experience what people of faith and wisdom

         have taught for ages.

The here and now is not just here and now.

Yes, it is that; but it is also much more.

When times of caregiving fill with richness and brim with vitality,

    often in ways that are unanticipated and unrepeatable,

        then these earthly experiences are infused with a bit of heaven.

They become remarkable experiences that ground you in living

    and root you in meaning.

They become reminders that while you're sharing in caregiving,

    others are engaged in similar acts elsewhere and everywhere.

Together you are participating in the grand dance of life

    with all the generations who have gone before you,

        and with all who will ever follow you.

And you recognize that it is not just you who acts,

    not just you who gives care and receives care.

A Presence acts through you, and in you,

    as well as apart from you.

And yours is the privilege of witnessing this each time you reach out,

    and each time someone—or Someone—reaches back.

After you had taken your leave,
I found God's footprints on my floor.

Rabindranath Tagore

We usually fail to see God
because we have forgotten
how to stoop low enough.

Jewish proverb

It is not necessary to have great things to do.
I turn my little omelet in the pan
for the love of God.

Brother Lawrence

Begin each day with quiet and prayer.

Take at least twenty minutes to address your spiritual needs and prepare for your day. Read writings of wisdom and passages of scripture and reflect silently on what stays with you. Take in those things that nurture your soul: poems, prayers, songs, sermons. Listen to sacred music, or sing it, or play it. Sit in protracted silence, listening for God's voice. Pray. Pray for the one in your care, for your caregiving, for others. Carry this time with you throughout your day.

Create a sacred space.

Somewhere in the area where you regularly work, make room for those objects, signs, or symbols that carry spiritual significance for you. A religious emblem? A piece of soulful artwork? A small table that holds meaningful mementos? Maybe a special candle? Ask the person in your care what they would like, and be sensitive to their desires.

Treat your caregiving as sacred.

Recall the words of Benedict of Nussia: "Treat all your tools and instruments as though they were sacred vessels of the altar." Treat all your caregiving aids and supplies (yes, all of them) as if they assist in life-giving purpose. Use these thoughtfully, gently, reverently. Approach your partner in care as nothing less than a sacred person. View your caregiving routines as rituals as well as chores.

NEVER FORGET: THERE IS A GRACE IN BEING A CAREGIVER.

Every caregiver experiences a call.

That call may come in the anxious voice of a family member or friend,

    or with an imploring look in their eyes,

        either of which says, "I need you. Will you help?"

The call may come through anonymous faces lined with suffering,

    both young and old, both near and far.

The call may be handed from one generation to another, like a trust;

    or from guide to pilgrim, like an honor,

        or from lover to loved, like a gift.

For some, the call is carried like a voice from above or beyond.

However it comes, the communication is the same:

    "You are wanted and needed."

However it is delivered, the question is implicit:

    "Will you respond?"

As you well know, it's not easy being a caregiver.

There are days when your energy runs low,

    when your spirit sags,

        when you anxiety peaks.

There are times when the hours are too long,

    when the demands seem too many,

        when the rewards feel too few.

There may be instances when the other is hard to care for—

    they may be angry or depressed and take it out on you;

        they may feel lost or forsaken

            and push away your efforts to help.

There may be periods when you feel unacknowledged or unappreciated,

    when you feel lonely and alone.

There may be times when what's expected seems beyond your abilities,

    when what's asked of you is more than you have to give.

It's true: being a caregiver has demands and difficulties,

    annoyances and adversities.

It has its full share of pain.

Yet being a caregiver is also deeply meaningful.

You can help a fellow being as you would want to be helped.

You can do for another what they could not do without you.

You may nurse them back to health and vitality.

You may accompany them to a place of calm and stability.

You may facilitate their journey from life on earth to life beyond.

But all this is only a beginning.

There will be times in your caregiving when you realize,

    however much the other has gained,

        you have gained just as much, perhaps even more.

In the act of accepting another, you will be accepted.

In the act of comforting, you will be unexpectedly comforted.

In the act of dying with another, you will be reborn.

There will be times in your caregiving when,

    however tired you are, you're ever so alive;

        however separate you feel, you're ever so connected;

            whatever brokenness you've known,

                you've never felt more whole.

Through the discipline of your caregiving,

　　you can experience what many before you have known:

In being a blessing for another, you are blessed.

In being a vehicle for growth, you grow.

In being a conduit for healing, you are healed.

And, in holding out the promise that, no matter what has happened,

　　transformation is still possible,

　　　　then you yourself can be transformed—

　　　　　　caregiver and care receiver alike.

And you will know that this transformation is not something

　　that either of you has accomplished,

　　　　for it comes from beyond you.

You will realize, if you have not already,

　　that you are cared for on the grandest scale possible.

And the most fitting response you can make is a prayer

　　that contains only four words:

　　　　"Thank you.

　　　　　Thank you."

Books by James E. Miller

When Mourning Dawns
A Pilgrimage Through Grief
How Will I Get Through the Holidays?
What Will Help Me?/How Can I Help?
Winter Grief, Summer Grace
One You Love Has Died
When You're Ill or Incapacitated/When You're the Caregiver
The Caregiver's Book: Caring for Another, Caring for Yourself
Welcoming Change: Finding Hope in Life's Transitions
When You Know You're Dying
One You Love Is Dying
When A Man Faces Grief/A Man You Know Is Grieving
Finding Hope: Ways to See Life in a Brighter Light
The Art of Being a Healing Presence
The Art of Listening in a Healing Way
Autumn Wisdom
Change & Possibility
This Time of Caregiving
My Shepherd Is the Lord
Effective Support Groups
The Rewarding Practice of Journal Writing
And others.

VIDEO PROGRAMS BY JAMES E. MILLER

Invincible Summer

Listen to Your Sadness

How Do I Go On?

Common Bushes Afire

By the Waters of Babylon

Why Yellow?

Nothing Is Permanent Except Change

We Will Remember

Gaining a Heart of Wisdom

The Grit and Grace of Being a Caregiver

Awaken to Hope

Be at Peace

The Natural Way of Prayer

You Shall Not Be Overcome

When Mourning Dawns

All Seasons Shall Be Sweet

My Shepherd Is The Lord

Still Waters

The Art of Listening in a Healing Way

This Time of Caregiving

And others.

James E. Miller is a writer, photographer, spiritual director, workshop leader, and speaker who creates resources and gives presentations in the areas of loss, transition, caregiving, healing presence, spirituality, and older age. He speaks before many professional groups and at various institutions, often incorporating his own award-winning photography in his talks. He leads workshops and conducts retreats throughout North America.

To discuss bringing him to your area, call 260.490.2222 or email *jmiller@willowgreen.com*.